CW00864668

The Krays

Britain's Most Notorious Gangsters

Roger Harrington

Part 1 – Childhood

London, East End, 1945.

The East End of London in the 1940s was a post-war landscape. Poverty and crime were rife. People struggled to make ends meet and opportunities to escape were few and far between.

Houses were cramped due to increased immigration and from the bombing during the war. Food was still scarce as rationing didn't end until 1954 and cheese production was slow for many years after. In addition to this the Suez crisis lead to a period of petrol rationing from late 1956 until May 1957.

All of this lead to a feeling of unease about people's futures. No-one knew where the next full meal was coming from. The black market was in full force, although this was not a new phenomenon.

The East End of London was a notorious breeding ground for criminals from as far back as the 17th century, so it wasn't limited to just the aftermath of the war causing social issues. The high levels of poverty in the area made it an easy way to make a living when jobs were scarce.

Some people resorted to collecting scrap to increase their income, while others resorted to less legal ways to achieve financial stability. Extortion rackets, muggings and random acts of violence made the streets of the East End a largely unsafe place. The streets became notorious for dangerous activity and the shadow of violence was always around the next corner.

Of course the notoriety didn't become a national sensation until the 1950s and 1960s, when arguably the most famous East End gangsters were plying their trade. Ronald and Reginald Kray - The Kray Twins.

Ronald and Reginald Kray, or Ronnie and Reggie as they came to be known, were born on the 24th of October 1933 to Charles Kray and Violet Lee. Reggie was the older of the two identical twins by ten minutes.

Born in Hoxton the twins moved to Bethnal Green in 1938. When the Second World War broke out, the twins' father was called up to the army and decided it would be better to go into hiding than join the front line.

The twins had an elder brother Charles junior, who was six when they were born, as well as a sister, Violet, who had died while still a baby.

Charles senior was rarely around while the twins grew up, as he worked as a travelling trader, buying and selling valuable metal and clothes as well as being in hiding due to being called up to the army. This lead to the twins being brought up by their mother, Violet.

Violet was a warm and compassionate woman, who in the absence of the twins' father dedicated her life to her children. Ensuring that they were always well dressed and trying to instil good values, respect and to make sure that they treated others less fortunate than themselves with compassion.

Other members of the family that lived in close proximity to the twins were their maternal grandparents, who lived over the road from the Krays, and their maternal aunts - Mary and Rose, who lived in the houses either side of them.

Rose was the twins' favourite aunt, possibly

because she indulged them, or possibly because her own violent temper mirrored what theirs' would eventually become. When Ronnie was teased at school about having eyebrows that were very close together, she thought it was an omen and told him he was "born to be hanged".

At the age of three, both Ronnie and Reggie suffered with a serious case of diphtheria. This was especially worrying as their younger sister had died as from a similar ailment as an infant. Fortunately, for Violet they both pulled through, although Reggie made a swifter recovery than his twin.

Their father would regularly visit the house while on the run, but with the police and army regularly calling upon the house his visits became less and less frequent. The twins attributed their father not visiting to the regular appearance of the men in uniform. This would later cause them to have a deep-seated disdain for such authoritative figures which they carried with them into their adult lives.

Their father had associated with many local East End criminals and this association - as well as their ingrained hatred for authority - had a significant influence on their later life choices. Especially with the feeling of being able to do no wrong that they got from the unconditional love their mother always showered them with.

The first school the twins attended was Wood Close School. The outbreak of the Second World War would break up their education and they were then evacuated to Suffolk. This, as well as their father going into hiding, made their childhood one of constant upheaval and uncertainty.

The Kray twins enjoyed living in Suffolk, but Violet missed her family. Eventually, she decided that they would all move back home. The twins were crushed, they went back to school and began to take become interested in boxing; a family tradition.

Their maternal grandfather, Jimmy Lee, was a former bare knuckle fighter. Their father, although he had dodged conscription, came from a long line of boxers and wasn't one to back down from a fight. Their brother Charlie taught them how to box, and their natural aptitude for physical violence became apparent.

Their father took them to the Robert Browning youth club for boxing lessons as often as he could and the twins progressed at a rapid pace to become very competent fighters.

In 1948 Reggie became the schoolboy boxing champion of London and reached the finals of the Great Britain schoolboy championships. Ronnie was similarly gifted although he didn't quite achieve the same accolades as his brother.

Charlie said the twins were very different fighters, with Reggie being more calculated and skillful and Ronnie always being all guns blazing and fighting until he couldn't fight anymore.

There are varying reports on how successful the twins were as amateurs. Some accounts say they never lost a bout, although the fact that Reggie did not win the Great Britain Schoolboy finals disprove this claim. In addition to this, they are said to regularly have fought each other, but there is no record of a result of such incidents. What is certain, however, is that the twins were very skilled fighters.

The twins eventually turned professional. They would later claim that a fight at a travelling fairground whey they were pitted against each other was their first professional bout, but as it was an unlicenced exhibition, the match didn't enter the record books.

Both twins were successful in the bouts they did compete in. Ronnie fought in six fights and managed to win four, Reggie, the more skilled of the two and with more amateur accolades, fought in six and won six.

The twins' brother, Charlie, was also an accomplished boxer. He kept a punching bag in his grandfather's house and regularly trained at the local boxing gym. In 1951, all three Kray brothers fought on the same bill, and Charlie was the only one to lose his fight. This would turn out to be his last fight, and it wouldn't be long until the twins ceased boxing altogether, although for very different reasons.

The twins didn't just keep their fighting in the ring. There was a lot of gang activity in the East End of London and the twins were willing participants in any kind of violence. They kept weapons on hand at all times as well as a cache of implements stashed in their bedroom.

At the age of sixteen, the twins were charged with GBH for a violent confrontation between two gangs. Although charged, the twins were acquitted due to lack of evidence. Some say that a character reference from a local vicar, who the twins ran errands for, helped them out immensely. Others feel that the witnesses had been "got to" and was persuaded to not testify in court.

At seventeen, the twins again found themselves in front of the courts. After Ronnie had an altercation with a policeman who had pushed him, both twins got involved in resisting arrest and were therefore charged with assault. Another helpful hand from the local vicar lead to them only receiving probation.

The trouble with the law had not stopped their boxing career, although a solid conviction may have. In fact, the story of the Kray twins could have been very different - with them being successful boxers - were it not for the next significant event in their lives.

It was the second of March 1952 that the twins were called up for national service. A two year military duty that was mandatory for all 18 year olds in England at the time. The twins thought that they could put up with the two years if the army allowed them to take on an easy role; something akin to fitness instruction was their intended role.

Unfortunately, this never came to fruition as yet another case of bad choices, bad luck and the dislike for uniformed authority figures reared its ugly head. They had an altercation with a training officer which lead to them running back home after they had physically attacked him. The police then arrested them the following day, and this event started a long two years either in hiding, or inside military prisons.

While on the run, the twins ran into yet more trouble with the law when they assaulted a police officer. This time they ended up in jail, albeit with no vicar to rescue them. A month in Wormwood Scrubs followed by them being sent back to the army to be court martialled. The Krays would then, yet again, stage a daring escape from military grounds. However, this time they were recaptured less than a day later and the rest of their national service was spent locked up at Shepton Mallet.

It was here, locked up at Shepton Mallet, that the twins met a different breed of men. Men more in tune with their attitude of disdain toward authority, and especially authority in uniform. One of these men in particular was Charlie Richardson, who the twins would come to have many dealings with in the future, culminating in becoming rivals in the gang scene in London.

After they were finally released from Shepton Mallet, the twins spent a year taking on small-time crime jobs. Odd jobs such as working in protection rackets and working as bouncers at the nightclubs owned by local criminals became their most common source of income. It was during these jobs where the Krays came up with their idea for the next stage in their advancement. They had ambitions of becoming bosses of the criminal underworld.

The twins elder brother, Charlie, loaned them some money to take on the lease of a run-down snooker club. It was a rough place, often the scene of multiple fights and regularly had broken glass covering the floor on the morning after a particularly raucous evening. The club was named The Regal which, before the twins took over, could be considered quite an ironic name for such an establishment. However, once the Krays took on ownership of The Regal, it suddenly became a club without trouble. Whether this was because of the fearsome reputation that the twins had cultivated, or because the twins were the ones who smashed it up so often is a question that will never be answered.

It was during this time that the twins began to take on the image of 'gangsters'. Smart suits, large rings and heavy watches all became part of their image. Even though the trouble had long since stopped at their club, the twins did nothing to dissuade the more undesirable elements of society from frequenting their establishment.

People who had been released from jail, old army friends, tough men and boys from the estate - the twins welcomed them all into The Regal with open arms. This allowed the twins to repel any type of protection racket being launched on their club. The one occasion such an incident did occur was when a Maltese gang attempted to extort the twins. The luckiest of the men simply had his hand speared with a bayonet, while the rest of the gang all left the club much closer to death than when they entered.

It was during their ownership of The Regal that the twins started to branch out into other areas of criminal activity. They hijacked lorries which had numerous desirable products loaded on them. With the black market still thriving in an only-recently post-ration Britain, there was both a ready supply and many customers for the twins' illicit goods.

The twins began to use The Regal as more than just a legitimate business. It became a front for their criminal activities. Local villains used the club as a meeting place to formulate plans, the back room became a storage area for stolen goods and the twins became a go-between for people to fence their stolen goods. Even if they themselves were not involved in the stealing of the goods, they still took a cut of any deal that took place on their premises.

The two young upstarts in the criminal world were beginning to make a name for themselves. More established gangsters were starting to notice their antics, most of the local crime bosses ignored them, but some were less than impressed.

The twins had attracted the attention of three brothers who worked on the docks. They were the established bosses of the area and they were not happy with Ronnie and Reggie cutting into their business. As is commonplace within the crime world, a cryptic message was sent to the twins. They were invited for a Sunday morning drink at the pub that the brothers regularly drank in.

Ronnie and Reggie knew that this would be the first test of their mettle in the criminal world, both mentally and physically. The twins arrived at the pub and entered the private bar. The three dockers were drinking, and all three were physically more intimidating than Ronnie and Reggie were. The twins closed the door behind them and proceeded to obliterate the three men in front of them. When the pub manager opened the door to see the aftermath, he was shocked to see two of the dockers out cold and one being brutally pummelled by Ronnie.

By 1956 the twins had begun to run an expanding criminal empire. At this point, the twins were still only 22 years of age and yet were running a section of the capital city of England. Ronnie helped to protect their fearsome reputation and Reggie was the brains behind their rapid expansion. They soon began to skim from the top of other criminals' earnings, taking a percentage of anything that was earned on the area that they ran.

During the twins rise up the ladder of crime, the East End of London had been run by two men: Billy Hill and Jack Spot. The pair had an uneasy alliance with one another and it was only a matter of time before their relationship would come to a head. When they eventually did fall out, Jack Spot was attacked and, in the aftermath of the attack, called on the twins for support. Ronnie and Reggie were only too happy to support Jack Spot, seeing this as an opportunity to both speed up their rise and learn from someone who was experienced in the ways of gangland crime.

The twins saw this as a real opportunity for them to graduate into the big leagues, but this all changed in May 1956 when Jack Spot was attacked again. This time it was outside his apartment, and was also in the presence of his wife. Jack's face was slashed and, due to his substantial injuries, decided to make a complete career change. Jack Spot then bought a legitimate furniture store and turned his life around with no criminal activity to speak of.

In a strange twist of fate, Billy Hill also decided to retire, which left an opening at the top of the crime totem pole. This left space which was soon filled with new gangs, either remnants of Spot and Hill's old gangs, or new ones who had decided to take advantage of a potentially explosive situation. The main worry for the twins was a gang of Italians who were rumoured to be targeting Ronnie and Reggie.

Deciding that attack is the best form of defence, the twins made plans to ambush the Italians at the social club they used as a base.

Driving there with various members of their gang, Ronnie stormed the social club. Once inside, he argued with the Italians before drawing his gun and firing in the club. Although no-one was wounded, his point had been made. The Kray twins were not to be trifled with. As Ronnie commented himself in later years "we weren't playing kids games anymore."

The twins began to transition into more serious crime. The Regal started to be used as a gang headquarters as well as a business and party zone. They removed the cavalcade of tearaways and hangers on that had been frequenting the club and replaced them with more ambitious criminals. People who wanted to take their life of crime seriously. They called themselves 'The Firm' and they became a who's who of the criminal underworld in London. One man who, notably, never managed to join the inner circle of The Firm was Jack 'the Hat' McVitie. Even though the twins didn't know it, he would go on to play a very big part in their lives.

The twins began to make an incredible amount of money and their turf covered a significant area of the East End of London. With the majority of the businesses, both legal and otherwise, paying a percentage of their earnings to the Kray twins, they could afford to live a lifestyle befitting of two successful gangsters.

It was during 1956 that Ronnie's unhinged behaviour and penchant for violence first became a serious problem for the twins in a business sense. A car dealer who had paid protection from the twins had trouble with a disgruntled customer. The customer was threatening to bring friends with him to extract a refund from the dealer. Ronnie dealt with the issue by shooting the disgruntled customer in the leg when he returned to the car dealer.

This lead to the victim of the shooting identifying Ronnie as the shooter, but when the police arrested him, he swore blind that he was Reggie and even had identification to prove it. Whether it was Ronnie or Reggie who was arrested is still a mystery to this day, but whoever the shooter was had Reggie's driving licence and was released without charge.

While all of this was happening, a fixer was employed to make sure that the problem went away. All people involved were made to promise their silence and the victim of the shooting was financially remunerated for his troubles.

This served only to add to Ronnie's sense of invulnerability that he had gained from his Mother's smothering as a child. It became a bone of contention between the twins; Ronnie constantly bragging of being untouchable annoyed Reggie as he felt angered that he had to clean up Ronnie's mess. He told him "you shoot a man, then leave me to clean up the mess. One day you'll get us hanged."

The twins' reputation as men who could sort out trouble was eventually what lead them to their first real bump in the road as criminals, and first shed a real light on Ronnie's mental health issues. A friend of the Kray twins, Billie Jones, had taken over a club that had a lot of issues with trouble. A situation that mirrored their own takeover of The Regal. The owner couldn't handle all of the trouble, especially as it brought the interest of the police down on the club. An associate of both Jones and the Krays, Bobby Ramsay, suggested that the twins come on board as partners. Although it would end up being a decision that would cost Ronnie dearly, they were happy to do so as in their eyes it was another revenue stream. A revenue stream that was, most importantly, a legitimate business.

Not long after this business arrangement, Billie Jones found himself involved in a dispute with a member of a gang from the docks. The gangs from the docks always had issues with the gangs from the rest of the East End of London. They were tough, and had easy access to items that they could steal coming through the dock. Jones came off worse in a fight with a gang member, this prompted Ramsay to get involved. As the altercations escalated, Ramsay ended up being beaten quite severely. This prompted Ronnie and Reggie to feel as though they had to become involved, after all, they were business partners of the two men.

Ronnie and Reggie set up members of the gang, targeting them while they were drinking in a pub. Unfortunately for the twins, details of their plan had got out to the gang. They all ran out of the back of the pub as the twins entered. Only one man failed to escape: Terry Martin. Bobby Ramsay identified Terry Martin as one of the men who had beaten him. He was then taken outside and almost beaten to death.

The twins were stopped that same night by a passing police car. Ronnie and Reggie were tried with GBH and Ronnie had an additional charge of carrying a firearm. Reggie managed to dodge the charges, but Ronnie was not so lucky and ended up being sent to jail for three years.

While Ronnie served his sentence, the fortunes of the twins could not have been more different. Reggie managed to grow their empire, both criminal and legitimate. The twins owned at least thirty businesses in the East End of London by the time Ronnie was finally out of prison.

Ronnie had always been the dominant twin, even though Reggie had a more keen business sense. Their differences had often cost them financially, however, now that Ronnie was in jail, Reggie could make more sound business decisions, allowing their empire to continue growing.

The Regency was scheduled to be knocked down by powers outside of the Krays' influence, so Reggie decided to move the location of their headquarters elsewhere. He settled on an abandoned shop. The Firm organised the decorating and within four months of Ronnie being sent to jail, Reggie opened his new club, named with his brother in mind, The Double R.

It attracted all manner of celebrities and rich clientele. Reggie finally felt he had made it. He wasn't just mingling with celebrities, he was now one himself. Charlie, the twins' brother, came back into his life. He made suggestions for Reggie to extend his legitimate business interests. Reggie was all too happy to take these on board and the Kray empire continued to grow.

Ronnie however suffered from much worse fortune. While in jail his mental health deteriorated at an alarming rate. He began to worry he was being targeted by unknown people. These delusions only intensified when he was moved to a prison on the Isle of

Wight, where no-one knew of his status and influence. The guards became worried for his well-being and kept watch over him to ensure he wouldn't hurt himself. This only made Ronnie more nervous.

He was diagnosed as suffering from 'prison psychosis', which at the time covered any kind of mental illness brought on by being locked up. He was medicated and seemed to be recovering, until he heard the news of the death of his Aunt Rose. She died on Christmas day 1957, Ronnie found out on the 27th. He became manic and had to be placed in a strait-jacket to stop him from hurting himself. On the 28th of December, his mother Violet received a telegram from the prison: "Your son Ronald Kray is certified insane."

Ronnie was diagnosed with schizophrenia, although the authorities were not completely correct with the diagnosis, after being transferred to a lunatic asylum in Surrey named Long Grove Hospital. While here, doctors noticed an improvement in Ronnie's condition, and the decision was made that he should stay at Long Grove rather than be transferred back to prison.

Ronnie was not happy with this decision and, by the end of May that year, he was desperate to escape. Luckily, Reggie had the perfect plan. On an allotted visiting day, the twins switched places. When the staff at Long Grove were finally aware what had happened it was too late; Ronnie was long gone. It was during Ronnie's premature freedom that Reggie realised he had made a big mistake.

The plan was for Ronnie to stay hidden for six weeks, because anyone who was outside for that long had to be reclassified, then Ronnie would hand himself over, be classified as sane and then serve the last of his term in regular prison. However, Ronnie couldn't handle this. He was becoming more and more paranoid by the day. He offered to kill the troublesome neighbour of the farmer whose land he was hiding on. He was taken back to the East End by Reggie and a doctor was brought in to help him settle. Ronnie was surviving on two bottles of gin and multiple tranquilizers a day. He was a mess.

Finally, Reggie realised his error of judgement. Even though the twins had a code of silence, Reggie broke that code in order to help his brother. He phoned Scotland Yard and they arranged to pick up Ronnie the next morning at 2am. Ronnie left with the police without even looking at his family. Reggie was distraught.

In a strange twist of fate, Ronnie only spent two more weeks at Long Grove. He was diagnosed fit to finish his sentence and finally in 1959 he was released from prison. The Krays were back together, but Ronnie was different and it spelled the start of their eventual downfall.

After Ronnie's release from prison, the difference in him was astounding. Not just in his attitude - he'd always been the more violent and short tempered of the pair - it was also clear from his appearance. His eyes were tighter, his jaw line had altered. He looked and acted, according to one report, like 'a demon'. He wasn't the intimidating man he used to be. Ronnie soon started to cause trouble for Reggie. It was most apparent when he threatened violence and demanded protection money from a gambling den that Reggie already owned.

The former financial security that Reggie had created was slowly becoming smaller and smaller. Their business interests barely covered their expenses. For all of Reggie's business acumen, Ronnie was equally as violent. It didn't help the business aspect of the Krays' empire. It did, however, make sure that they stayed just as feared as ever.

Ronnie was dragging the twins down, but it was Reggie who made the next mistake. The twins made friends with a car dealer named Daniel Shay. Shay attempted to extort a local shopkeeper with the twins in tow. When the trio left, the shopkeeper called the police. When Shay and Reggie went back to collect the money, they were both arrested. Shay was sentenced to three years in jail and Ronnie eighteen months.

This gave Ronnie exactly what he longed for. He no longer had Reggie to curtail his more violent plans. He could finally do what he always wanted. He could go to war. He had already acquired the nickname Colonel, now he finally had a war to fight, and troops to command.

He started by targeting Peter Rachman. Rachman was a slum lord in Notting Hill, which was not the elite metropolitan area it is known as today. Rachman resisted paying protection money, but knew that he would never get out from under Ronnie's protection racket if he started paying. He needed something else, and he found it when the government made the decision to legalise gambling.

Rachman knew Stefan De Faye, who owned Esmerelda's Barn which was in a very upmarket area of London (not far from Buckingham Palace). A meeting was set up, which Reggie was able to attend as he was out on bail, and the twins were joined by their friend Leslie Payne. De Faye agreed to sell his shareholder in the club but stay on as an executive and manager to run the club.

The club was an absolute gold mine for the twins. They made almost £100,000 a year from their shareholding in the club, which, in the early 1960s, was an incredible sum of money (it would be the equivalent of earning £1.6 million in 2017 as a frame of reference).

Unfortunately for Reggie, his appeal failed and he was sent back to prison just after Christmas that year. It was a bad thing for Ronnie too, as he soon began to lose control of his finances and his behaviour. He had gained a taste for the high life from being a regular socialite. Just as Reggie had when he opened the Double R, Ronnie started associating with celebrities. He also made a number of bad choices that impacted Esmerelda's Barn.

Ronnie took huge markers that bounced. The manager of Esmerelda's Barn offered Ronnie £1000 a week just to stay away from the club. Ronnie refused, he didn't care about the money. He loved the lifestyle. He used his money and fame to sleep with young men, of any creed or colour, Ronnie was proud that he was without prejudice. Regardless, he still craved violence. A clairvoyant told him that he was a reincarnation of Atilla the Hun and he would achieve greatness through violence and then die young. Ronnie's violent tendencies may have calmed down, but they didn't go away.

The influence of Leslie Payne caused the business interests of the twins to explode beyond their wildest dreams. They used what they called the "long firm" fraud. They would open a business and run it by the book. When they had the trust of suppliers they would place large orders on credit, sell the items at any price and then the business would vanish without a trace, leaving creditors wondering what had happened.

Payne set up a legitimate business operation with an accountant to cover their shady domestic and international deals. It was around this time that Ronnie thought he had found what would be his ticket to immortality.

He met Ernest Shinwell, the son of a famous politician. Shinwell was involved in building a village in Nigeria. Ronnie saw this as the act of philanthropy that would catapult him to greatness. There was a lot of interest from the Nigerian government but their issue was financing.

The Kray twins decided to invest their own money in the project. Unfortunately, there were some less-than-scrupulous people involved in the deal. Payne was detained in Nigeria and the twins had to bail him out. Ronnie was crushed at losing his opportunity for immortality. His rage began to become uncontrollable.

He started thinking of new ways to punish people who crossed The Firm, to the point that he openly mentioned castrating people. Reggie struggled to control Ronnie's violent urges. A boxer had his face slashed by Ronnie which resulted in the boxer requiring over 70 stitches, all stemming from the Nigerian deal collapsing.

Part 2 – Murders & Victims

The man who was involved with the first meeting between Ronnie and Lord Boothby, Leslie Holt, died under very strange circumstances. It is rumoured to have been one of the Kray Twins first murders, but is by no means confirmed. Surprisingly, for two with such a violent career and how quickly they climbed the ladder of crime, Ronnie and Reggie were only ever convicted of two murders.

The first murder that it is known they committed was that of George Cornell. Despite all of Ronnie's anger issues around this time, it wasn't this that caused the murder of George Cornell. The cause was the rumblings of a gang war between The Krays and a gang south of the River Thames, The Richardsons.

When a known Richardson associate "Mad" Frankie Fraser worked his way into taking some gambling machines that the Krays owned, Ronnie was not happy. As a response they tried to take a slice of an extortion racket that the Richardsons were running at Heathrow car park. When this didn't happen, they were waiting for a moment for revenge, but in the end it wasn't even all of this that caused them to kill George Cornell.

There was already heat between the twins and George Cornell after he had told the twins to back off over the extortion racket, Cornell a former member of The Firm, had switched sides when he got married, was a large intimidating man. Not afraid of anyone, or of handling any business he needed to, in any way.

He was drinking in a club named Mr Smith's on March 8th 1966. He was with other members of the Richardson gang; Frankie Fraser, Harry Rawlings, Ron Jeffries, Jimmy Moody and their boss Eddie Richardson. The club was owned by two men from Manchester and the Richardsons handled both club security and the gambling machines on the premises.

The club didn't just hold drinkers from one gang. It was host to a number of gangs from the south of London. On this particular night there was a gang of men drinking there that included Richard Hart, a cousin of the Kray twins. The trouble which later ensued that night was not related to the gangs being rivals, however. Billy Hayward, a man drinking with Richard Hart had been having an extramarital affair with the mechanic for the Richardson gang. Fearing retribution for his indiscretions, he began shooting at the men from the Richardson gang on the other side of the pub.

Harry Rawlings was shot through the shoulder, Frankie Fraser and Eddie Richardson were both wounded by bullets and Richard Hart was shot dead. This shoot-out ultimately lead to the breakup of the Richardson gang, as many of the men involved were arrested and sent to prison.

Even though the police arrested most of the people involved in the shoot-out, the Kray twins took the death of their cousin, Richard Hart, as a personal insult. The rumours that were flying around the East End of London were that George Cornell was the man who fired the shot that killed Richard Hart. Ronnie and Reggie wanted revenge and they didn't have to wait long to get it.

The very next day, George Cornell was drinking in a pub named The Blind Beggar. Ronnie, Reggie and The Firm were in a pub named The Lion not far away. An unknown assailant phoned The Lion and informed the twins of Cornell's whereabouts. The twins took two of The Firm with them and made their way to The Blind Beggar to confront George Cornell. The two men were John Dickson and Ian Barrie – their driver. They drove to the pub and pulled up right outside.

As Ronnie and Ian Barrie walked into the pub, George Cornell gave them a submissive glance and remarked with a sarcastic snarl "Well, look who's here now". Ronnie walked right up to the bar where Cornell was sat, pulled out his gun and shot him in the head three times. Ian Barrie fired his gun into the ceiling as the bar staff and customers all ducked for cover. Cornell collapsed and hit a pillar, one of the bullets hit the jukebox, forcing it to stick on the track that was playing. Ironically, the song was titled "The Sun Ain't Gonna Shine Anymore". It didn't for George Cornell.

While the initial motivation for the murder of George Cornell was the death of Richard Hart, it was also rooted in Ronnie and Reggie needing to keep control of The Firm. If they hadn't taken action after the death of one of theirs at the hand of another gang, then they would have looked weak and may have lost control of their own. While the rumours did say that Cornell was the one that shot Richard Hart, it was also a matter of Cornell being the only one who wasn't in jail. Added to all of these factors that Cornell had been bad mouthing the Krays, it could have been any one of these factors that made them take the decision to shoot George

Cornell, or was most likely the combination of all of them.

Scotland Yard assigned the case of finding Cornell's killer to Superintendent Butler, but was hindered from the start. All witnesses to the crime denied having seen anything, with the barmaid even going as far as being unable to identify Ronnie in a line up. Ronnie went free but he wasn't as confident as he had been when he had escaped arrest. Rumours of fresh evidence being found scared the twins and they ran off to Morocco until they were thrown out by the chief of police for being undesirable aliens.

Although they had gotten away with the first murder they committed, the second one was the one that proved to be their undoing. After the killing of Cornell, Reggie had been trying to reconcile with his wife Frances. They booked a holiday together in Ibiza, but tragically, Frances committed suicide shortly after. Now it was Reggie's turn to descend into a pit of depression and poor mental health. He began drinking heavily and started to make rash, violent decisions that were completely different to his usual cool demeanour. Reggie became like Ronnie; twisted, mean and very dangerous.

He shot two people, albeit only wounding them. He sliced a man's face open with a knife and two members of The Firm vanished while a third who tried to leave was left a funeral wreath on his front door. While there is no concrete evidence about what happened to the two members of The Firm who disappeared, Reggie Kray claimed on his deathbed that he had been denied parole because of his involvement in another killing in addition to what he had been arrested for. This is thought to be "Mad"

Teddy Smith, although it has never been proven.

Ronnie always wondered why his brother didn't seem to have it in him to kill someone. Ronnie spent a lot of time bragging about how he had shot George Cornell and got away with it. Reggie always seemed to stop short of killing, and Ronnie never understood why. When Reggie finally did decide to cross the line and kill someone, it was crossing that line that was finally the undoing of the Kray twins empire.

Before they got to the man that proved to be their undoing, they sprung an old prison friend from jail with the intention of gaining media attention for his case and hopefully getting it reinvestigated. The man was Frank Mitchell "The Mad Axeman" who had broken into an old couple's home and held them up with an axe. He was a large man and had a history of mental illness. He was not unlike Ronnie in this respect. After he was broken out of prison the aim was for Mitchell to give himself up to the police once media attention had been gained. Unfortunately, it never got to that stage.

In late December 1966, Frank Mitchell was killed. The exact details of the murder are unreliable, but Freddie Foreman admitted in his autobiography that he had shot Mitchell. Their reasoning behind shooting Mitchell was that he had become too much of a problem. They couldn't handle his short temper or his refusal to give himself up.

It was decided that Mitchell had to be taken care of before the twins were implicated in his escape from prison. Albert Donoghue told Mitchell he was being moved to a safehouse in the countryside, but once he got Mitchell in the back of his van Foreman and another man shot him to death. According to Foreman they dumped his body in the English Channel, but was never recovered.

The twins were eventually charged with the murder of Mitchell, but there was not enough evidence to prove that they either had anything to do with it, or that they carried it out themselves. The Mitchell situation brought more attention to the twins, but it wasn't the final nail in their careers as criminals, that elusive honour goes to the decision to murder Jack "The Hat" McVitie.

Jack "The Hat" McVitie was an associate of The Firm, although he was not a fully-fledged member. He was nicknamed "The Hat" because he reportedly never removed the hat he used to hide his bald patch (according to some reports, even when he took a bath). He was different to the other members because he had no real respect for Ronnie or Reggie, and he certainly didn't fear them. He regularly carried out jobs for them, without becoming part of the inner circle.

It first became apparent that his uses might not outweigh the problems he created when he reneged on a deal to kill the twins' former business manager Leslie Payne. The twins were worried that Payne was going to talk to the police to avoid a charge hanging over his head. Ronnie paid McVitie one hundred pounds to kill Payne, with the promise of a further four hundred to be paid once the job was done. Jack McVitie didn't do the job, and not only did he not do it, but he also refused to pay back the deposit Ronnie had given him in advance. Ronnie was not happy about this, and he marked it in his mental scorecard.

The next time McVitie had a mark against him was after a day of drinking. McVitie stumbled into the 211 Club, which happened to be owned by an associate of the Krays, Billy Foreman. While in the 211 Club, McVitie threatened to wreck the whole place. This again angered Ronnie and pushed him closer to taking action against him.

Jack McVitie's third and final strike came when he threatened to owners of The Regency Club with a sawn-off shotgun. John and Tony Barrie, the owners, were both associates of the twins. This caused not only Ronnie to be past the point of no return, but even Reggie too. Even though Reggie was still in his downward spiral at this point, he was still more measured than Ronnie and he also found McVitie's actions a step too far. He knew something had to be done before he did some real damage, either to their earnings or to their reputations.

They decided to set a trap for Jack The Hat. On October 28th, 1967 the twins were drinking at The Carpenter's Arms with a number of their associates. A rumour among the local people was that a party was going to be happening later in the evening at a house owned by a woman named Carol Skinner, or "Blonde Carol". As luck would have it she also lived with a man who worked for the Kray twins.

While in The Carpenter's Arms a member of The Firm, Tony Lambrianou, introduced the Krays to friends of theirs from Birmingham; twins named Tony Mills and Alan Mills. They just so happened to be good friends with McVitie. They met up with him and a Kray associate Ronnie Hart in The Regency, and when the men from Birmingham suggested an after-hours party, Jack The Hat was only too happy to agree.

The men got into a car and made their way to Blonde Carol's house where Reggie and Ronnie had been clearing guests away for around an hour. When they pulled up just before midnight, there was only two of Ronnie's lovers and a man named Ronnie Bender at the house. Ronnie Hart, the Mills twins and Jack McVitie entered the flat. As McVitie entered the room Reggie walked right up to him, pointed his gun at his head and fired. Almost like a precursor for things to come, the gun jammed. Ronnie began screaming in McVitie's face while his lovers and the Mills twins ran from the house. Reggie began pushing and shoving McVitie across the room. McVitie tried to escape from a window but Reggie pulled him back in.

Jack McVitie was now standing in the room, without his hat, sweating profusely and looked visibly afraid; the first time he had ever been afraid of the Krays, "Why are you doing this, Reg?" he asked. He didn't get an answer, Ronnie just kept screaming at Reggie to kill McVitie. Reggie complied with his brother, he grabbed a knife from Ronnie Bender and stabbed it into McVitie's face just below his eye, then stabbed him in the chest repeatedly. Finally he stuck the knife through McVitie's throat, pinning him to the floor. That final stab almost symbolising the death of the Kray family as well as the literal death of Jack "The Hat" McVitie.

Finally dead, McVitie's body was wrapped in bedding and placed in Ronnie Bender's car. Tony Lambrianou drove it away, followed in another car by Ronnie Bender and Tony's brother Chris Lambrianou. Even though they were told to dump the body in the East End, they decided instead to dump it in Richardson turf to try and lay the blame at their feet. When the Krays found out, they became worried. They thought the blame may have been laid at the feet of their associate Billy Foreman rather than the Richardsons.

They phoned their brother Charlie who drove across London and made arrangements with Freddie Foreman, Billy's brother, and Ronnie Hart to have the body disposed of, and they did. Jack "The Hat" McVitie's body has still not been found to this day.

After the murder Reggie Kray said "I did not regret it at the time and I don't regret it now. I have never felt a moment's regret." In hindsight, he should have. This murder was what finally stopped the Krays' reign of terror, and what caused them to spend almost all of the rest of their life in prison.

Part 3 - Accomplices

Part of Ronnie and Reggie's success as criminals was their associates, who they referred to as The Firm. When they first started out, they used a collection of waifs and strays to carry out their dirty work, but as the progressed up the ranks of crime, they more and more surrounded themselves with hardened criminals.

Using people more inclined to a life of crime yielded much more success for the twins. While The Firm was not always organised, Ronnie and Reggie knew they always had reliable people who would be willing to take on any task. The first of these men was Albert Donoghue.

Albert Donoghue was an integral part of the Kray's day to day lives. He was Ronnie Krays personal minder for a while. It could have all been so different though, as on one of their early meetings Albert said something out of turn and Reggie Kray shot him in the leg as a punishment. When Donoghue said nothing to the police about the shooting it earned him a place in The Firm.

Donoghue was a part of many of the Krays most famous exploits, including helping to keep Frank "The Mad Axeman" Mitchell placid by taking supplies to him. On the night that the Krays ordered Freddie Foreman to kill Mitchell, it was Donoghue who lured him into the van to get shot, then Donoghue helped to keep the girl who had been staying with Mitchell placated by spending the night with her.

Donoghue eventually had a big part in the downfall of the Kray twins, when he refused to take the fall for the murder of Mitchell. He thought that he was to be next and he testified in court against the twins when they finally went a step too far.

Ian Barrie was another member of The Firm who played an important role in both the Krays day to day life, but also their downfall. A tough man from Glasgow, Ian Barrie was the man that Ronnie Kray used as his right hand man when he murdered George Cornell. Ian was loyal and worked hard for the Krays, usually the man that Ronnie would turn to the most, after Reggie of course.

Ian Barrie not only accompanied Ronnie Kray into the pub when he shot George Cornell, but he also ensured that no-one did anything that might cause them trouble when he fired his warning shots. The other member of The Firm to accompany Ronnie on the murder of George Cornell was "Scotch" Jack Dickson.

Jack Dickson usually worked as a driver for the Krays. He was a loyal soldier and did whatever was needed to keep their empire ticking over. However, Jack's loyaly was tested towards the end of his relationship with the Krays, when he found out that the they intended to persuade him to take the fall for the murder of George Cornell. Jack later testified against them in court.

While Ian Barrie never turned against the twins, he did do jail time for his involvement in the killing of Cornell. After his release from jail in the 1980s, Ian Barrie disappeared. No-one knows to this day what happened to him or even if he is still alive.

Pat Connolly, Big Tommy Brown, Billy Donovan, Connie Whitehead, John Barry, Sammy Lederman, Dave Simmonds and Nobby Clark were all members of The Firm who first became part of the group when the

Krays bought their first club The Regal. It was during this time that the first transition from young, tough children being the main part of the Kray gang to tough, criminal men being the main aspect.

John Barry, in addition to being a member of The Firm also owned The Regency club with his brother. They were paying protection money to the Krays, who also acted as silent partners in the running of the club. It was at The Regency that Jack McVitie put one of the nails into his coffin after his numerous antics, including threatening to shoot a man, stabbing someone and wiping the knife on a woman's dress and threatening to shoot both Barry brothers. This caused John Barry to complain to the Krays about the actions of McVitie.

These men all formed the basis of the muscle of the Kray gang. Carrying out all manner of extortion and intimidation to ensure that the Krays rose to the top of the pyramid of the gangs in the East End of London. Many of them started after leaving jail or if they were just down on their luck. The Krays believed in helping people to get on their feet. They believed that this kind of criminal philanthropy would result in greater loyalty from their underlings.

Chris and Tony Lambrianou were two brothers who were part of The Firm. They were two of the Krays most trusted and loyal members, and are most well known for their part in the murder of Jack "The Hat" McVitie. They played an integral part in getting McVitie to move on to the house of Carol Skinner, using their friends the Mills twins who were in turn friends with McVitie. In addition, they were in attendance when the murder took place, and then helped with the moving of the body.

The Lambrianou brothers ended up being two of the most loyal members of The Firm, as they didn't testify in court against the Krays when they were finally caught out and charged. They also served 15 years each for their part in the murder of Jack McVitie.

Ronnie Bender worked as a driver for the Krays. Another loyal member of The Firm, he never betrayed their confidence. He worked as a driver for them most commonly, and was involved in the disposal of McVitie's body. He attempted to leave the body on a railway line so that a train would destroy it, but was unable to fit the body in the boot of his car and so had to drive McVitie's car with the body on the back seat. He didn't testify against them in court, maintaining his loyalty to the twins, and ended up serving a life sentence for his involvement in the murder of McVitie.

Part 4 – Arrest & Evidence

The Krays criminal empire was far reaching across the majority of the East End of London by 1967. They hadn't paid much thought to the interest in them from Scotland Yard, but it was about to become a very serious issue. An issue that would end their careers as criminals, and their lives as free men.

After being promoted to the "murder squad", Detective Superintendent Leonard "Nipper" Read was given the task of bringing the Krays to justice. Having tried in the early 60s, but coming up against political opposition and the famous East End silence, Read was more than familiar with the illegal activities of the Kray twins.

Leonard Read was the perfect candidate to go after Ronnie and Reggie. He had been promoted to Detective Inspector at a very young age of 36 and had done so with his talent and hard work, rather than political machinations. By the time he was 43 he had been promoted to Detective Superintendent and was officially recognised as one of the top 12 detectives in the whole of England. This time, he would not be denied his convictions.

He had noticed that Scotland Yard didn't seem to spend much time or effort in attempting to bring down the Kray twins. It infuriated him that the top people had almost given up on ever stopping them. Whether that was due to their skills at avoiding the law, or due to greased palms is unknown. He set about building his team to bring them down.

By mid-1967 he had brought in John du Rose, head of the Murder Squad,

Superintendent Harry Mooney, Superintendent Don Adams, and Chief-Inspector Frank Cater. These men became the basis of the squad to apprehend the Krays. With an additional fifteen staff members they were well manned and had all of the resources they needed to finally bring an end to Kray twins reign as the heads of The Firm.

Read called a meeting of his team, he told them that they would have a deadline on their investigation of three months. Read was slightly optimistic on this deadline as it would take slightly longer than that to finally take the twins down. Their first port of call was to try to gather information from the people of the East End. It didn't garner any useful results. The code of silence prevailed and the Kray squad had to try a change of tack.

In the midst of all of this, Leonard Read had been ensuring that his men had been training for the possibility of a physical confrontation with the Kray gang. He had been making his men practice with the use of a handgun. Just like is the case now, the English police didn't regularly use handguns. He wanted to make sure that if it came down to a fire fight his men would not be outclassed by the Kray gang who were all proficient in the use of firearms. Additionally, they had to make sure that they changed their travel routes daily and their family members were prepared for if anything untoward happened.

Read's first port of call was a man named Alan Bruce Cooper. Cooper was being used as a source from within Scotland Yard and had employed a man named Paul Elvey, who was involved in three failed attempts at murder. When he was arrested and his link to Cooper revealed, Read found out about him being a high level source and attempted to use him as bait. Unfortunately the Krays didn't take the bait, and Read had to go back to the drawing board for a new plan.

Read made a choice that he would not be able to get the Kray twins on their current activity, and instead would have to focus on their past indiscretions. Read decided that the best form of attack would be to isolate weak links in The Firm. Read got thirty names and wrote them down in a black notebook. He called this his "delightful index".

Read and du Rose started investigating the legitimate businesses under the Krays' empire; mainly nightclubs and betting shops which acted as fronts for their illegal activities and places where they could launder money. It was at this point that the

Kray squad realised that they would have to both approach and rely on in court, criminals, to get the evidence and testimony they would need to send the Kray twins to jail. The police higher ups were initially resistant to this approach.

Read and du Rose became involved in a heated discussion with the top brass at Scotland Yard, including the police lawyers, but eventually managed to convince them that the testimony of criminals would be important in the case. At first they had very little luck, with one man telling them "I hate the sight of blood, especially my own."

Finally, Read and his team had a breakthrough. Leslie Payne got word to Read. He wanted to talk. Payne had been aware of the plan for Jack "The Hat" McVitie to murder him. He was also aware of the fact that McVitie had vanished after he had failed to kill him. Payne knew that he had to protect himself from the Krays, and knew that the underworld wouldn't be willing to help him. He knew he had to turn to the law, and so he did.

After Read got in touch with him, he was taken to a hotel in Marylebone. Here Payne stayed for three weeks, telling Read and his team everything that he could remember. In all he filled over two hundred pages of notes about the twins illegal activities. From violence and racketeering to their long term frauds, Leslie Payne detailed everything that he knew. By Christmas 1967 Nipper Read had a large database of information about the Kray twins and their illegal empire, and now all he needed was proof and witnesses to finally take them down for good.

By January 1968 Read and the rest of his team were tirelessly chasing down the leads that Leslie Payne had given them. The investigation took them across all of Europe and even as far as the United States at one point. Nipper Read and his team were working twenty four hours a day, seven days a week. They left no stone unturned in their pursuit of Ronnie and Reggie Kray.

Ronnie and Reggie were keeping a low profile during this time. Their own sources had told them that the police had begun to gather evidence against them. While they were not worried, they also didn't know how much information that the police actually had on them. Bizarrely, Ronnie bought himself a python at this point, going so far as to name it Read.

It was around this time that Ronnie bought a Victorian mansion and achieved a lifelong dream of becoming a country squire. It was here that the twins began to spend most of their time. While their criminal earnings were severely limited by the increased police scrutiny, they were still working on their plans, although now they were obviously no longer using Leslie Payne as their business manager.

During April Ronnie travelled to New York. There, he met up with a selection of gamblers, boxers and small time criminals. Although Ronnie did meet with two of the Gallo brothers - a crime family who were waging a war with the New York mafia - he didn't meet with anyone of real importance, and no serious plans were made on his trip.

Alan Cooper was the man they were using at this time as their business manager. They were completely unaware that Cooper was not only informing for Scotland Yard but was also working for the US treasury after he had been caught on a gold smuggling trip.

All of this information was not known by the Krays, so when Ronnie planned with Cooper to restructure the way The Firm worked, mainly to be more in line with how the American mafia was, he didn't know that this information was being passed on to Scotland Yard. It was at this time that Ronnie decided to assassinate certain important people in order to gain more respect from the American crime families and possibly build up a better working relationship.

He instructed Alan Cooper to sort out the supplies needed for a car bomb, as he felt this way would be the most impressive. Cooper used Paul Elvey for the task of procuring the explosives, but Elvey was arrested on his way back to London. During interrogation, he gave up Cooper and it was at this point that Nipper Read found out about Cooper being an informant for

Scotland Yard. It was now that Read had a difficult choice to make: charge him as an accessory, or release him and use him as a witness. Read went with the latter.

On May 8th Read brought his team together for one last meeting before they made their move. The plan was to strike first thing in the morning on May 9th. Armed officers were to arrest the twins and twenty four members of The Firm all at the same time. It had to happen simultaneously at twenty four different addresses to ensure that no-one could tell the others about the operation.

The need for all people to be arrested at once was to ensure that potential witnesses couldn't be coerced. As this was the way the Krays had managed to get out of all previous arrests, it was a very real possibility that they would use this tactic again.

Once all the teams were ready they began the operation. The twins were both with lovers when their door was smashed in. Ronnie with a young boy and Reggie with a young girl. Neither had any idea what was going on when they were arrested. Luckily for the police, the handgun training hadn't been needed.

All in all, only two of The Firm had managed to avoid capture: Ian Barrie and Ronnie Hart. It was feared that the case would fall apart as witnesses became aware that they may be targets, but the pair were quickly apprehended and the case went ahead.

On July 6th the twins had their preliminary hearing. It was here that Ronnie and Reggie first realised just how much trouble they were actually in. A member of their crew, Billy Exley, arrived to give evidence against the Krays. He knew a lot of their inner secrets and information on their long term frauds. Billy being there was a bad sign for Ronnie and Reggie. Added to this the barmaid from the night George Cornell was killed agreed to be a witness. Although she had been unable to identify Ronnie in a line up at the time, the promise of police protection and a new identity she was more than happy to point out Ronnie Kray and Ian Barrie as the two men who had entered The Blind Beggar pub on the night George Cornell was murdered.

The Krays were kept on remand until the actual trial, and Read was constantly worried that they would be able to get to witnesses. After eight months on remand, the trial began in January 1969.

The biggest surprise and possibly the most hurtful betrayal from all of The Firm was that of Ronnie Hart. Ronnie Hart was the twin's cousin, and had been involved in many of their illegal activities for a long time, most notably the slaying of Jack "The Hat" McVitie. The betrayal by Hart cut the twins deep, and had a lasting effect on Ronnie Hart too. He later attempted to commit suicide, although failed. After this, he emigrated to Australia.

Even though Ronnie and Reggie Kray had been running their criminal empire for over a decade, they were only tried for the murders of George Cornell and Jack McVitie. This was partly down to their skills at hiding their tracks and the code of silence that was prevalent throughout the East End of London. The trial lasted for two months, and on the 8th March 1969 the Kray twins were sentenced to life in prison, with the judge recommending that they serve no less than thirty years in prison.

Other members of The Firm that were sentenced included their brother Charlie, who got ten years for accessory to the murder of Jack Mcvitie. Ian Barrie received a life sentence for his part in the Cornell murder. Four other members of The Firm, including the Lambrianou brothers, Ronnie Bender and Albert Donoghue, were also sentenced at the same time as the Krays.

Finally, after months of work, Read had caught his men. The Krays' reign of terror over the East End of London was over. Ronnie and Reggie had run a successful if disorganised empire for more than ten years, and in the end were only convicted of two murders between them. This was a much more surprising incident than the fact that their career as criminals were finally at an end.

Part 5 - Legacy

While the Kray twins have had a lasting legacy and effect on popular culture in the world, and England especially, their legacy is especially felt in the East End of London. It is still a hotbed of crime to this day. Almost as soon as the Krays were jailed more gangs popped up to take their place.

Detective Sergeant Harry Challenor of the Flying Squad, the division of the police that the television series "The Sweeney" was based on, once commented:

"Fighting crime in London was like trying to swim against a tide of sewage; you made two strokes forward and were swept back three. For every villain you put behind bars there were always two more to take their place."

Harry Challenor was right, criminals didn't see their rivals being arrested as a deterrent, they saw it as an opportunity. The more criminals that were locked up, the more new ones sprouted up to take their place. The East End of London is seemingly destined to always be a place that attracts opportunistic villains who want to make their fortune off the hard work of others.

Almost as soon as the Krays were put away, The Dixons took on their business interests. When The Dixons were gone, The Tibbs came and went. Bertie Small, The Arif Family, The Legal and General Gang, the Knight Family, the list could go on forever. And unfortunately, it seems that it will.

Not only did new gangs pop up constantly, but two of the men who were most responsible for bringing down the Kray twins, John du Rose and Leonard "Nipper"

Read fell out of the picture. John du Rose, who became known as "Four Day Johnny" due to how fast he solved his cases, retired from Scotland Yard and Read moved North to become the Deputy Chief Constable of Nottingham police. These two men not only had a huge part to play in the Krays arrest and conviction, but they also had an aura that seemed to make criminals keep a lower profile. With them out of the picture, the criminals became a lot braver and a lot more brazen.

This is not to say that crime had never been an issue in the East End, it had always had a crime problem long before the Kray twins. What the Kray twins did was glamourize it; normalize it. People like to romanticize about their era. In the East End, it is common to hear people comment how certain crimes, like muggings of the elderly, wouldn't have happened in Ron and Reg's day. It doesn't occur to them that this normalisation of their criminal activities is partly what encourages the modern day criminal to follow this path.

Part of the romanticizing of the criminal lifestyle and the assertion that things were better then is also perpetuated by criminals of the time, like Tony Lambrianou who said:

"The East End was a hard place, it became famous for turning out gangsters. There was a better class of criminal in those day, there were rules you lived by, and if you broke them, you paid the price. Back when I was doing it, the code was this: You don't grass on your own mates. Ever. You respect women. You never steal off your own. The violence was among ourselves, or between us and people who knew our rules. If anyone was dealing with us, they were shady to begin with and they knew the score. The streets were safer when we was around, because no one in their right mind would come into our area and commit crimes. People don't respect life like we used to, or even respect themselves. I mean look how people dress. We may have been villains, but we always looked sharp."

The last line the most telling of all, as though being well dressed excused their behaviour.

Ronnie and Reggie Kray appearing with celebrities and being well known even by the general public in England was one of the first examples of criminals using the newspapers and media to legitimize what they did. Not only this, but they portrayed themselves as legitimate businessmen, so when the police did come down on them, they found it easy to play the victims.

Ronnie and Reggie Kray are an anomaly in

this world. They did terrible things to a lot of people, but they are still spoken about with great fondness. Part of this is down to the influence of their Mother. She instilled the trait of helping those down on their luck. Ronnie especially could not help himself when it came to helping those less fortunate, and he especially liked to help people just released from prison. These traits made a lot of people forget their indiscretions and lead to them being falsely remembered as heroes of the East End, rather than the vicious, ruthless and cruel criminals that they really were.

One of the biggest examples of this fondness in the East End came in 1995 when Ronnie Kray died. On March 17th of 1995 Ronnie Kray suffered a heart attack. Most likely caused by years of excessive smoking, Ronnie had smoked at least 100 cigarettes every day of his adult life, not to mention spent much of his time in smoky clubs. Reggie and the twins elder brother Charlie sorted the funeral between them and arranged it for the 29th March.

On Wednesday 29th March 1995 Ronnie Kray's funeral was held at St Mathews in Bethnal Green and was buried at Chingford Cemetery, which was six miles away. This cemetery was chosen because the twins Father, Mother and Reggie's wife Frances were all buried there. No expense was spared for the funeral and it cost £10,000. Thousands of people lined the streets from St Mathews in Bethnal Green, for the whole six miles to the cemetery.

The fact that all these people lined the streets, over twenty five years after the twins arrest and incarceration, shows the legacy of the Kray twins as well loved figures. In addition to this their funeral was attended by many gangsters from the era of the Krays, Frankie Fraser, Freddie Foreman, Johnny Nash and Teddy Dennis were all there, showing the respect the Krays held in the underworld, even almost 30 years after their involvement in it.

Another example of their lasting legacy was the death of their brother Charlie. On April 19th 2000, Charlie's funeral was held. Much like Ronnie's, thousands of people lined the streets. At 11am, Reggie Kray arrived at the funeral, handcuffed to a police officer, he was greeted by cheers and applause. Cheers and applause as though he was a war hero or film star, not a former criminal who had spent the previous thirty one years in jail.

On October 1st, Reggie Kray died of bladder cancer. His funeral was the biggest of them all. Police from six districts were called in to help control the crowd along the nine miles of road for the funeral procession. Ronnie had married in prison, and his wife Roberta threw a red rose into his grave; the same grave Ronnie had been buried in. The Krays had finally had their last influence on the East End, but as is apparent to this day their legacy was far from over.

The Krays legacy didn't just fall on the East End. They used their fame to sell books. The first book they wrote they wrote together and was released in 1988. Although the twins were credited as writers of the book, thirteen of the chapters were written by their ghostwriter Fred Dinenage. The second book, *Born Fighter*, written solely by Reggie Kray.

Born Fighter was written without the aid of a ghostwriter and tells Reggie's story of what happened while he and Ronnie ran their criminal empire. Released in 1990, it was very successful and brought the story of the Krays to a whole new generation of people. Helping to keep them in the public eye and making sure that their constant campaigning for release wasn't forgotten about.

Two years before he died, Ronnie released another book entitled *My Story*. Written as a sequel to the joint autobiography that he and Reggie had released in 1988, My Story told the story of many of his and Reggie's criminal activities as well as giving an insight into Ronnie's battle with mental health. It showed a slightly more sympathetic side to Ronnie Kray; one where he talked about being bisexual, how he hated being in Broadmoor and, although he didn't say it explicitly, his lack of understanding of his own mental illness.

The final book released by either of the Kray

twins was entitled *A Way of Life: Over Thirty Years of Blood, Sweat and Tears* in the year 2000 and was written entirely by Reggie. This book was a move away from talking about their criminal career and spoke at length about Reggie's time behind bars. By its time of release, Reggie had spent almost half of his life in jail in total and not only did he feel like he had served his punishment, but his repeated requests for release had all been turned down. It wasn't until he was diagnosed with terminal cancer that he finally gained his release for a short while before he died.

The books written by the Krays weren't the only examples of literature about their criminal career. Countless books have been written about their criminal enterprise, as well as being written by various members of both members of The Firm and by members of rival gangs.

Maybe the most famous book about the Krays is *The Profession of Violence* by John Pearson. Different from most of the books written about the Krays, it was written by a man who was actually contacted by the twins and asked to write their biography. Well researched and endorsed by the twins, *The Profession of Violence* was so well received and not written just to cash in that it ended up being made into a very successful film.

Krays-related media has almost become a sub-genre of the crime genre itself with most books about gangsters being linked to the Kray twins in some fashion. Their name being linked to a book automatically gives it credibility, especially for some of the unknown villains who didn't make enough money from their criminal career, and so try to supplement their pension with tall tales and sometimes outright lies.

It's not just the world of literature that the Krays' legacy and influence has extended to, the music industry has also used their name in its output, although not as shamelessly as the publishing houses of the world. Artists as diverse as Blur, The Libertines, Morrissey and Ray Davies of The Kinks have all referenced the Krays in their song lyrics.

Of course, those artists mentioned didn't need a rub from the Kray twins in order to sell records. They were either already established or had enough talent that they would make it there in the end regardless. One such band who didn't fall under this category was a band named Renegade Soundwave, whose first single was entitled *Kray Twins*. Although they did have roots in the East End, it was still an attempt at cashing in on the notoriety of the Krays, and while they did achieve some degree of success, they never managed the longevity of the other artists who used the Krays in their songs.

While the Krays were never officially named in the titles of any plays, they were used as the basis for two plays in the 1970s. *Alpha, Alpha* in 1972 was the first play that was loosely based on the lives of the Kray twins. It never achieved mainstream success, although it perhaps would have if the title had explicitly mentioned them by name.

The second play to use Ronnie and Reggie as a basis for their story was *England, England;* a musical which was first debuted in 1977. Similarly to *Alpha, Alpha* it never achieved mainstream success. It received higher praise than *Alpha, Alpha*, partly due to having Bob Hoskins in the lead role providing some star power. Just like *Alpha, Alpha* we'll never know if a specific mention of Ronnie and Reggie would have helped it to achieve more success, given how it helped book sales.

Not only are the Krays still a huge influence on literature, they play a big role in the film world. Before mentioning the numerous films about the Krays, their influence and legacy is telling in almost every British gangster film - Guy Ritchie in particular being very influenced by the lifestyle, image and mystique of the Kray twins. *Lock, Stock and Two Smoking Barrels* and *Snatch* both borrow their imagery heavily from the way the Krays dressed and carried themselves. As well as the imagery, Ritchie himself has admitted to being heavily influenced by the 1970 film *Performance*.

Performance is an important film for cinema in general. Guy Ritchie isn't the only director who is influenced by it. Quentin Tarrantino wears the influence heavily on his sleeve in *Reservoir Dogs* and *Pulp Fiction*. While it may seem at first the film isn't directly influenced by the Krays, the main character in the film is a bisexual gangster from the East End of London. While that similarity may seem enough to show that it is at least partly based on the life of the Krays, there is more to prove it.

The lead role of Chas, was played by the actor James Fox. While he was researching for the role, to ensure he played it to the best of his ability he met with Ronnie in prison to gain an insight into how he thought and why he acted the way that he did. *Performance* wears its influence very obviously, the Krays legacy extends even to films not directly related to them.

The first actual film about the life of the Krays was the 1990 film entitled simply *The*

Krays. The film starred brothers Gary and Martin Kemp, of the new romantic band Spandau Ballet, as the Kray twins. While the film does cover the violent and ruthless aspects of the twins' lives, it focused more on their interactions with their Mother and with each other. The screenplay, written by Philip Ridley, utilised some creative storytelling, particularly the dialogue of their Mother which reportedly infuriated the real Ronnie and Reggie.

They were not happy about the way their Mother cursed in the film. They said that she never cursed in her life. They also felt that Martin and Gary Kemp were not intimidating enough to play them. They felt that they 'weren't scary enough', especially given their past in a new romantic band. The critics, however, didn't feel the same. It won numerous awards and was nominated for a number of others. While the critics felt the film was of a good quality, it didn't resonate as well with the public. The film never received a wide release at cinemas and only grossed $2 million at the box office.

It was another twenty five years until another Kray film was released: *The Rise of the Krays*. It didn't go down the usual route of glamorizing the life of Ronnie and Reggie. Instead, it portrayed them in a very realistic light. It showed their cruelty, their evil nature, and ultimately the unstable criminals that they actually were. While many people thought that *The Rise of The Krays* was quickly put together to capitalize on the high budget mainstream movie, *Legend* starring Tom Hardy, it was actually in production before Legend was announced and was simply a coincidence that both films were released in the same year - not a cash in to ride the coattails of the bigger budget film.

Legend was a big budget blockbuster released in 2015. Starring Tom Hardy as both Ronnie and Reggie Kray, it received mixed reviews upon its release, and was based on the previously mentioned well-received book by John Pearson. There is a lot of inaccuracies in most films that get the big budget treatment, but the most glaring one in this is Reggie's treatment of Frances. While Reggie was undoubtedly a violent man, people who knew him knew that he had great respect for women. He was profoundly against violence against women and the way he was portrayed treating Frances in Legend who certainly have provoked an angry reaction from him if he was still alive.

Not only was it out of Reggie's character to do anything violent to Frances, she insisted many times that Reggie was never physically violent towards her; a claim which was backed up by friends. The film changes the type of abuse portrayed in Pearson's book, from psychological to physical. According to Pearson he regularly threatened to kill her and her family, but never physically harmed her in any way.

The playing down of the part the twins' Mother, Violet played in their lives would not have gone down well either if either of the twins were still around today. Their Mother was an integral part of their lives, someone that they not only loved dearly but looked up to and respected. The first film biopic incurred their wrath after it portrayed their Mother cursing, this one downplaying her influence in their lives would have been greeting with just as much vitriol.

While *Legend* did well at the British box office, grossing over $20 million, it didn't do so well in America. Maybe this speaks volumes for their influence in England, as opposed to overseas. In England, they were, are and probably always will be a big deal, whereas in America they fall under the radar because they can't compete with American anti-heros in terms of violence and infamy.

The final film biopic to date about the Krays is *The Fall of the Krays* in 2016. A low budget sequel to *The Rise of the Krays* from 2015. It was met with almost universally bad reviews. It was a film served no real purpose, especially with the previous year having had two films about the Kray twins released. While the first film was an honest attempt at making a biopic about the pair, this film was considered to be nothing more than a shameless cash-in.

Conclusion

That fact speaks volumes about the lasting legacy of the Kray twins. Although they were vicious, brutal and cruel killers, Ronnie and Reggie Kray both had charm and charisma that captivated people. Their story still interests people, seventeen years after the death of Reggie Kray, and almost fifty years after they were jailed. The Kray twins have a big appeal, especially in England.

While their effect on the East End of London doesn't physically bear their name, it is their legacy. London will never be the same because of Ronnie and Reggie. Their biggest success though, is that their name is still seen as a draw by the entertainment industry. Even after their death, Ronnie and Reggie still have the capability to make money. It's just that these days, it's for other people and a lot less people get hurt. Ronnie and Reggie Kray may well have been criminals, but their names are something that very few can forget.

Printed in Great Britain
by Amazon